画述孔子

*intings of Confucius*

············ 中英对照 ············

吴冰（泮墨）/ 编绘

山东城市出版传媒集团·济南出版社

图书在版编目（CIP）数据

画述孔子 / 吴冰编绘 . -- 济南：济南出版社，
2022.10

ISBN 978-7-5488-5229-2

Ⅰ . ①画… Ⅱ . ①吴… Ⅲ . ①孔丘（前 551- 前 479）
—生平事迹—通俗读物 Ⅳ . ① B222.2-49

中国版本图书馆 CIP 数据核字（2022）第 191331 号

出 版 人　田俊林
责任编辑　许春茂
装帧设计　宋英敏
出版发行　济南出版社
地　　址　山东省济南市二环南路 1 号（250002）
编辑邮箱　393305802@qq.com
发行电话　（0531）82924885　67817923
　　　　　　　　　86131704　86131701
经　　销　各地新华书店
印　　刷　济南鲁艺彩印有限公司
版　　次　2022 年 10 月第 1 版
印　　次　2022 年 10 月第 1 次印刷
成品尺寸　185 mm × 260 mm　1/16
印　　张　6.5
字　　数　60 千字
定　　价　48.00 元

# 前　言

　　《画述孔子》全书由两部分构成：画述孔子生平事迹、画述孔子故乡遗迹风情。

　　画述孔子生平事迹展示的主要是人物画，对每幅画采用"一句儒家名言 ＋ 一个孔子故事"的形式进行阐释。这样的处理方式便于读者了解"画中事"，读懂"画中理"。在这一部分内容中，作者还展示了春秋时期的一些冠饰、服饰、生活用具等，有助于读者了解那个时代的社会风貌。

　　画述孔子故乡遗迹风情展示的主要是风景画。画作主要呈现了孔子故乡曲阜的一些文化遗迹与风土人情。这部分内容可以帮助读者深入探索孔子生平和研究儒家文化。

　　本书为中英双语版本，在英译的过程中主要参考了英国汉学家理雅各、中国翻译家辜鸿铭先生翻译的国学经典著作。

　　由于编写人员水平有限，书中难免存在疏漏之处，恳请读者批评指正。

# Preface

The book *Paintings of Confucius* consists of two parts: "Paintings of Confucius' Life Deeds" and "Paintings of the Relics and Customs in Confucius' Hometown".

"Paintings of Confucius' Life Deeds" mainly shows figure paintings. To interpret each painting, we adopt the form of "a famous Confucian saying with a story of Confucius". It will facilitate its readers to learn about the stories in the paintings and understand what they want to tell the audience. In this part, the author also shows some crowns, costumes, and living utensils of the Spring and Autumn Period in the paintings, which helps readers understand the social style of that era.

"Paintings of the Relics and Customs in Confucius' Hometown" mainly shows landscape paintings. Those paintings mainly show some cultural relics and customs in Qufu, the hometown of Confucius. This part can help the readers to learn about the life of Confucius and study Confucian culture.

This book is a bilingual version of Chinese and English. Part of the translations are from the classics of Chinese studies translated by the British Sinologist James Legge and the Chinese translator Mr. Gu Hongming.

Due to the limited capability of the writer, there might be omissions in the book. Sincerely, suggestions and criticisms are welcomed.

# 孔子

　　孔子，名丘，字仲尼，春秋末期鲁国人。孔子生于公元前551年9月28日，卒于公元前479年4月11日，是中国古代著名的思想家、教育家，儒家学派创始人。

---

# Confucius

　　Confucius, whose given name was Qiu and courtesy name was Zhong Ni, was a native of the State of Lu in the late Spring and Autumn Period. He was born on September 28, 551 BC and passed away on April 11, 479 BC. He is a famous thinker, educator, and founder of Confucianism in ancient China.

# 目录　Contents

## 画述孔子生平事迹
## Paintings of Confucius' Life Deeds

## 画述孔子故乡遗迹风情
## Paintings of the Relics and Customs in Confucius' Hometown

# 画述孔子生平事迹

*Paintings of Confucius' Life Deeds*

# 惟德动天 ——《尚书》

只有道德的力量才能感动上天。

Only virtue can move heaven.

—*The Book of History*

# 麒麟送子

　　相传，孔子出生前空中飞来了一只口衔帛书的麒麟。帛书上写着"天遣奎星下凡，以振周朝"。麒麟出现后，颜徵在感觉腹痛。这时，天上的仙翁和乐齐鸣，并高声呼喊着"天降圣人"，没过多久孔子就出生了。麒麟送子的传说一直流传到了今天，在孔子的故乡，贴麒麟窗花、写麒麟对联庆祝家中有孩子出生已经成为一种习俗。

# Kylin Delivering the Sage

　　It is said that before Confucius was born, a kylin came with a silk manuscript in its mouth, on which it said, "The heaven will send the Great Kui the Star Prince down to the earth to invigorate the Zhou Dynasty." Whereafter, Yan Zhengzai went into pains of delivery. And at this time, the immortals in the sky started to sing with music and cry：Heaven will send the sage to the world. Before long, Confucius was born. The legend of kylin delivering a child has been handed down to this day. In the hometown of Confucius, it has become a custom to paste window decorations and couplets with the theme of kylin to celebrate the birth of children in the family.

# 物有本末，事有终始 ——《大学》

每样东西都有根本有枝末，每件事情都有终结有开始。

Things have their roots and their branches. Affairs have their end and their beginning.

—*The Great Learning*

# 夫子洞

这是关于孔子诞生的另一个传说故事。

公元前 551 年，孔子在夫子洞中出生。孔父见刚出生的婴儿长相太丑陋，于是将他遗弃在洞中。孔母颜徵在非常伤心，来到夫子洞寻找孔子。她惊讶地发现，一只老虎正在给洞中的婴儿喂乳汁，一只老鹰正拍打着翅膀为婴儿扇风。

# The Fuzi Cave

This is another legend about Confucius' birth.

Confucius was born in a cave in 551 BC. His father saw that the baby was too ugly, so he abandoned the baby there. Confucius' mother, Yan Zhengzai, was very sad and came to the cave again to look for her child. She found in surprise that there was a tiger nursing the baby and an eagle flapping its wings to fan him.

# 穷则独善其身，达则兼善天下 ——《孟子》

　　在不得志时，要注意提升个人的品德修养；在得志时，要使天下人都得到好处。

　　If poor, they attended to their own virtue in solitude; if advanced to dignity, they made the whole kingdom virtuous as well.

*—The Book of Mencius*

# 孔子放牛

孔子和母亲居住在鲁国都城曲阜时，生活极为艰难。孔子说："吾少也贱，故多能鄙事。"所谓"鄙事"，应该是指放牧牛羊、吹鼓、做农活等。孔子大概 7 岁时进入齐国晏婴的乡学接受启蒙教育。乡学结业时，他已经知道了五礼、六乐、五射、五御、六书、九数等知识。

# Herding Cattle

When Confucius and his mother lived in Qufu, the capital of the State of Lu, they lived a tough life. Confucius said, "When I was young, I lived a poor life, and I made my living by doing something humble." Something humble refers to manual labor, such as herding livestock, playing instruments, farming, etc. When Confucius was about seven years old, he entered Yanying's village school in the State of Qi and received elementary education. By the time when he graduated, he had learned five types of ritual, six styles of music and dance, five ways of archery, five methods of horsemanship, six structures of written characters, and nine types of mathematics, and so on.

# 积善之家，必有余庆 ——《周易》

积善行德的家庭，必然会有享受不完的喜庆。

The family that accumulates goodness is sure to have superabundant happiness.

—*The Book of Changes*

# 孔子结婚

公元前 533 年，19 岁的孔子亲自迎娶宋人之女亓官氏为妻。孔子主张，哪怕是王孙贵胄，在成亲的时候也应该穿上冕服，亲自去女方家里迎接新娘。亲自迎接新娘代表着新郎会用饱含敬慕的感情和新娘相亲相爱。孔子的这一主张开创了男方去女方家里迎亲的婚俗，并且这一婚俗延续至今。

# Wedding Custom

In 533 BC, at the age of 19, Confucius married a Qiguan, whose family lived in the State of Song. Confucius advocated that even the royal lords should dress formally and go to the bride's house and escort the bride back to groom's house in person, which means the groom would love the bride with admiration and respect. This idea of Confucius created a marriage custom, which continues to this day.

# 仁者，人也 ——《中庸》

仁爱就是爱人。

Benevolence is the characteristic
element of humanity.
　　　　——*The Doctrine of the Mean*

## 命名荣贶

公元前 532 年，亓官氏为孔子诞下一子。鲁昭公听说后，赐鲤鱼表示祝贺。孔子感到莫大的荣幸，于是给儿子取名为鲤，字伯鱼。

早在春秋时期，鲤鱼就有了祥瑞之意。在"鲤鱼跃龙门"的传说故事中，黄河鲤鱼只要能够跃过龙门，就可以变成真龙。

# Name After the Gift

In 532 BC, Confucius' wife, Qiguan, gave birth to a son. When Duke Zhao of the State of Lu heard about it, he congratulated Confucius with a carp. Confucius felt so honored that he named his son Li and gave his son a courtesy name, as Boyu. In Chinese, the "carp" sounds like "Liyu" or "Li".

The custom of using carp as auspiciousness was already popular in the Spring and Autumn Period. For example, in the legend of "carp leaping over the Long Men", as long as the carp in the Yellow River can leap over the Long Men, it can become a loong.

# 君子欲讷于言而敏于行 ——《论语》

君子说话时要谨慎，行动时要敏捷。

The superior man wishes to be careful in his speech and agile in his conduct.

——*The Confucian Analects*

# 孔子做官

　　结婚后，孔子在鲁国给季氏家族管理粮仓。官职虽小，但工作一点儿也不好干。因为各诸侯国的度量衡制度不同，要精通各国的制度，还要在工作中不出现差错，实在是太难了。但孔子却把这份工作干得很好。

# Serving in the Court

　　After Confucius got married, he managed the granary of the Ji family in the State of Lu. Although the official position is minor, it was not easy to do this job. Because the system of weights and measures varied among the vassal states, to be proficient in the national system and make no mistakes in the work was pretty hard. However, Confucius did his job very well.

# 大乐必易，大礼必简 ——《礼记》

大乐一定是平易的，大礼一定是简约的。

The great music must be ease, and the great rite must be simple.

—*The Book of Rites*

# 孔子学琴

相传，孔子 29 岁时拜师襄子为师，学习弹奏古琴。 孔子学琴非常认真，一连十几天都在练习同一首曲子。师襄子几次劝孔子更换练习曲目，但他不同意，因为他希望通过乐曲去感受曲作者的性格、长相等。一天，孔子告诉师襄子，他练习的那首曲子的作者应该是周文王。师襄子听了非常惊讶，因为孔子练习的正是周文王所作的《文王操》。

# Learning to Play Guqin

It is said that Confucius learned to play Guqin under the guidance of Shixiang at the age of 29. Confucius learned very seriously, and practiced the same tune for more than ten days. Shixiang advised Confucius to practice another tune, but he refused because he wanted to feel the character and appearance of the composer through music. One day, Confucius told Shixiang that the tune he practiced was composed by the King Wen of the Zhou Dynasty. Shixiang was surprised to hear this because the tune Confucius practiced was exactly *"King Wen Cao"*, written by the King Wen of the Zhou Dynasty.

# 学而不思则罔，思而不学则殆 ——《论语》

学习而不思考会迷惘无所得，思考而不学习会陷入困境无所获。

Learning without thought is labor lost; thought without learning is perilous.

——*The Confucian Analects*

# 杏坛设教

孔子说自己三十而立，这是因为30岁的孔子在治学、做人、为政等方面都已经有了明确的目标。据说，孔子每到一个地方都会在杏林里弦歌讲学，休息时就坐在杏坛上。后来就有人把孔子讲学的地方叫作"杏坛"，现在"杏坛"是教育圣地的代名词，泛指聚众讲学的场所。

# Teaching at Xing Tan

Confucius said that at his thirties he was able to think for himself and had a clear goal in study, behavior, administration, etc. It is said that wherever Confucius went, he would give lectures in the apricot grove and sat on the altar in the apricot grove to rest. Later, people called the place where Confucius gave lectures "Xing Tan". In Chinese, Xing is the pronunciation of apricot and Tan is the pronunciation of alter. Now "Xing Tan" is a synonym for the holy land of education and also refers to the place of giving lectures.

# 礼之用，和为贵 ——《论语》

礼的作用，以遇事都做得恰当为可贵。

In practicing the rules of propriety, a
natural ease is to be prized.

—*The Confucian Analects*

# 问礼老聃

老子曾在东周朝廷担任文官，管理过藏书。孔子听说老子博古通今，懂得礼乐的根本，明了道德的宗旨，于是和弟子南宫敬叔赶赴东周洛邑拜见老子，向老子请教中国古代传统礼制的问题。老子给孔子讲了许多如何为官、做人的道理，让孔子受益匪浅，终生难忘。

# Consulting Lao Tzu About Ritual System

Lao Tzu once served as a civil official in the Eastern Zhou Dynasty, managing the collection of books. Confucius heard that Lao Tzu was erudite and informed, knew the foundation of rites and music, understood the purpose of morality, so he and his disciple Nangong Jingshu went to Luoyi to pay a formal visit to Lao Tzu. Confucius wanted to consult Lao Tzu about the ancient traditional ritual system. Lao Tzu told Confucius a lot about how to be an official and a person, which benefited Confucius and made him memorable in life.

# 知者乐水，仁者乐山 ——《论语》

有智慧的人喜欢水的品格，有仁德的人喜欢山的品格。

The wise find pleasure in water; the virtuous find pleasure in hills.

—*The Confucian Analects*

# 孔子观水

孔子喜欢看水，子贡曾问他，为什么一见到水就要驻足观赏。孔子说："那大江大河的水是多么了不起的存在啊，它们哺育生灵有德行，和顺温柔有情义，从无惧色有志向，荡涤万物施教化。水的德行这么好，当然要观赏啊。"孔子还常借水来体悟人生，他曾在河边发出慨叹："逝者如斯夫，不舍昼夜。"

# Running Water

Confucius liked observing running water. Zigong once asked him why he stopped to watch the running water as soon as he met it. Confucius said, "What a remarkable existence the great river is for it's virtuous in nurturing living beings, gentle and affectionate, aspirational and fearless, and cleansing everything. That's why I love observing the running water." From it, he learned to understand life and nature. Once Confucius sighed by a stream, "Time passes by like this, flowing day or night."

# 满招损，谦受益 ——《尚书》

自满于已取得的成绩会招来损失和灾害，谦虚反而能得到益处。

One loses by pride, and gains by modesty.
——*The Book of History*

# 观器论道

孔子带着弟子们拜谒鲁桓公的庙堂时，在庙堂内看到了一个悬挂着的器皿。孔子说："这是欹器，水少时它是倾斜着的，水适中时它是正立着的，水一满它就会翻倒。"弟子们取水来试了试，果真如孔子所说。孔子感叹道："怎样才能盈而不覆呢？做人做事一定不要骄傲自满。"

# Observation and Truth

When Confucius led his disciples to pay a visit to the temple of the Duke Huan of the State of Lu, they saw a vessel suspended on a shelf. Confucius said, "This is a warning container. If there is little water, it will be slantwise. If the water is appropriate, it will be upright. And if filled with water, it will be overturned." Later, the disciples tried, and it turned out as Confucius had said. Confucius sighed, "How can things be full without overturning? You should always be moderate and never be conceited and complacent."

# 差若毫厘，缪以千里 ——《礼记》

　　虽然开始时只有一点误差，但是结果却是千差万别。

A millimeter miss is as good as a thousand miles.

—*The Book of Rites*

# 矍相圃比射

据史书记载，孔子不仅满腹经纶、孔武有力，还精通射箭。孔子观看乡射礼时曾发出感叹："听着音乐还能射中靶心的人，一定是品德高尚的贤人，那些品德不好的人怎么可能射得中呢！"后来，孔子带着弟子们在矍相圃练习射箭，来围观的人多得好像一堵墙。轮到子路和序点时，孔子让他们邀请一些品德高尚的人来比射，结果只有寥寥数人符合参加比射的条件。

# Shooting at the Garden

According to historical records, Confucius was not only knowledgeable and physically strong but also proficient in archery. Confucius once sighed when he watched the archery, "Those who can hit the bull's-eye while listening to the music must be the people of virtue. How can those people with bad morals hit the target!" Later, Confucius led his disciples to practice archery at the Garden with many onlookers. When it came to the turn of Zilu and Xudian, Confucius asked them to invite some people of noble character to compete. However, only a few people met the conditions.

# 为政以德，譬如北辰 ——《论语》

用道德来治理国政，自己便会像北极星一般。

He who exercises government by means of his virtue may be compared to the north polar star.

— *The Confucian Analects*

# 苛政猛于虎

孔子和弟子们去齐国途经泰山时，看见一名妇人在一座坟墓旁哭得非常伤心。孔子让子路去询问妇人为何如此。妇人说："我公公、我丈夫都死于老虎之口，现在我儿子也被老虎咬死了。"孔子问："那你们为什么不搬离这里呢？"妇人说："因为这里没有繁重的徭役和赋税。"孔子听后非常痛心，他对弟子们说："你们要好好记住，苛政猛于虎也！"

# Tyranny and Tiger

When Confucius and his disciples went to the State of Qi via Mount Tai, they saw a woman crying miserably by a grave. Confucius asked Zilu to ask what happened to the woman. The woman said, "My father-in-law and my husband had been killed by the tiger before, and later my son was also bitten to death by it." Confucius asked, "Why don't you leave here?" The woman answered, "Because there is no heavy corvee and taxes." Hearing this, Confucius said to his disciples in sorrow, "You must remember that tyranny is fiercer than the tiger!"

# 大乐与天地同和 ——《礼记》

大乐与天地自然和谐。

The great music is in a natural harmony
with heaven and earth.

—*The Book of Rites*

# 闻《韶》忘味

　　孔子 36 岁时在齐国听到了优美的《韶》乐。《韶》乐是歌颂舜帝德政的音乐，韵律优美，曲风平和。孔子称赞《韶》乐"尽美矣，又尽善也"，并学了起来。据说孔子学习《韶》乐时沉醉其中，以至很长一段时间食肉不知肉之味。

# Taste of *Shao*

　　At the age of 36, Confucius heard the *Shao* music at the State of Qi. The *Shao* is the ancient music praising the virtues of Emperor Shun, with grace in rhythm and harmony in style. Confucius praised *Shao* for its perfection, so he learned it. It is said that Confucius was so fascinated when he learned *Shao* that he couldn't taste the meat for a long time.

# 君子博学于文　　——《论语》

君子广泛地学习文化知识。

The superior man extensively studies all

learning.

　　　　　　　　　—*The Confucian Analects*

# 商羊知雨

一天，一只看上去只有一只脚的鸟落在了齐国的宫廷内，并舒展着翅膀跳跃。齐景公见了觉得很奇怪，于是派人问孔子是否认识这种鸟。孔子说："此鸟名叫商羊。民间有'天将下大雨，商羊跳起舞'的说法，商羊出现意味着不久就会有水灾。我们要赶紧告诉百姓这个消息，让他们挖渠修堤。"果然，没过多久就大雨倾盆，很多诸侯国都遭了水灾，只有齐国得以幸免。

# Shangyang and Flood

One day, a one-legged bird landed in the court of the State of Qi, stretching its wings and dancing. The Duke Jing of Qi felt very strange, so he sent a man to ask Confucius about the bird. Confucius said, "The bird is called Shangyang. There is a folk saying that 'as long as Shangyang appears and dances, it will rain heavily'. We should tell people to dig canals and build embankments in case of flood as quickly as we can." It rained heavily soon after, and all states suffered from floods except Qi.

# 克己复礼为仁 ——《论语》

克制自己的私欲，使言行举止合乎礼
节，就是仁。

To subdue one's self and return to
propriety, is perfect virtue.

—*The Confucian Analects*

# 受鱼致祭

　　在孔子去楚国的途中，有位渔夫想送给孔子一条鱼，但被孔子婉言谢绝了。渔夫说："因为天气炎热，鱼已经卖不出去了，与其把它扔掉我还不如把它送给你。"孔子听了再三拜谢并收下了鱼。随后，孔子让弟子们把地打扫干净，准备用这条鱼祭祀。弟子说："这本是渔夫打算扔掉的鱼，您为何要用它祭祀？"孔子回答道："我听说致力于施舍而不随便糟蹋的人是圣人，我们既接受了圣人的赏赐，又怎能不祭祀呢？"

# Sacrificing Fish

　　When Confucius was on his way to the State of Chu, a fisherman wanted to offer him a fish, but Confucius refused. The fisherman said, "It is so hot that the fish is unsaleable. It's much better to give it to you than throw it away." After hearing this, Confucius thanked him and accepted the fish. Later, Confucius asked his disciples to clean up the ground and prepare to sacrifice the fish. A disciple said, "It is what the fisherman planned to throw away. Why do you sacrifice it?" Confucius replied, "I've heard that those who prefer handing things out to wasting them are saints. Since we have accepted the saint's gift, how can we not sacrifice it?"

# 敏而好学，不耻下问　　——《论语》

　　天资聪颖又好学的人，不以向地位比自己低、学识比自己差的人请教为耻。

He was of an active nature and yet fond of learning, and he was not ashamed to ask and learn of his inferiors.

——*The Confucian Analects*

# 孔子拜师

相传，春秋时期莒国有个名叫项橐的男孩儿智力超群。孔子途经莒国时看见项橐用土在路上筑了一座"城"，于是就从一旁绕了过去。项橐见了问他："你为何放着城门不走，偏要绕过去？"孔子解释道："你筑的'城'非常好，我怕把它踩坏了。"项橐说："城若不让人走，要它有何用！"孔子觉得项橐很有想法，于是邀他同行。通过交谈，他发现项橐不仅才华过人还深知孝道，于是提出拜项橐为师。

# Acknowledging a Boy as His Teacher

According to legend, during the Spring and Autumn Period, in the State of Ju there was a boy named Xiang Tuo who was so intelligent. When Confucius was passing through the State of Ju, he saw a "city" built by Xiang Tuo on the ground, so he walked aside. Xiang Tuo asked, "Why did you go around the 'city' instead of through it?" Confucius explained, "The 'city' you built is perfect, and I don't want to destroy it." Xiang Tuo said, "The 'city' is made to be walked through." Confucius considered Xiang Tuo was a clever boy, so he invited Xiang Tuo to travel with him. Through the conversation, Confucius found that Xiang Tuo was talented and filial to his parents, so Confucius proposed to acknowledge Xiang Tuo as his teacher.

# 不学礼，无以立 ——《论语》

不学习礼，在社会上就很难立足。

If one does not learn the rules of propriety,
one's character can not be established.

—*The Confucian Analects*

# 过庭诗礼

孔鲤是孔子唯一的儿子。一天，孔子正立于庭院中，孔鲤从院中走过。孔子问他："你学《诗经》了吗？"孔鲤回答："没有。"孔子说："不学《诗经》，就不知道如何与人好好交流。"于是孔鲤开始学习《诗经》。

又一天，孔子立于庭院中，孔鲤从院中走过。孔子问："你学礼制了吗？"孔鲤说："没有。"孔子说："不学礼制，就不知道如何立身处世。"于是孔鲤开始学习礼制。

# Teaching at Courtyard

Kong Li was the only son of Confucius. One day, Kong Li passed through the courtyard while Confucius was standing there. Confucius asked him, "Have you learned *The Book of Poetry*?" Kong Li replied, "Not yet." Confucius added, "If you do not learn, you will not be fit to converse with." Therefore, Kong Li started to learn the book.

Another day, Kong Li met Confucius in the courtyard again. Confucius asked him, "Have you learned the rules of propriety?" Kong Li replied, "Not yet." Confucius added, "If you do not learn the rules of propriety, you will not know how to conduct yourself in society." Therefore, Kong Li started to learn the rules of propriety.

# 子帅以正，孰敢不正 ——《论语》

做领导的以身作则，行为端正，他手下的那些
人，有谁敢不行为端正呢？

If you lead on the people with correctness, who will
dare not to be correct?

—*The Confucian Analects*

# 中都宰垂钓

　　51 岁那年，孔子进入政坛，出任鲁国中都宰。为官期间，他尽职尽责，勤于政务。经过他短短几年的治理，中都百姓安居，社会安定。相传，孔子政事之暇喜欢垂钓，"子钓而不纲"说的就是孔子喜欢钓鱼，但从来不用网捕鱼。孔子仁义，他用自己的实际行动教育弟子们凡事要懂得节制，要适可而止。

# Leisure in Zhongdu

　　At the age of 51, Confucius entered politics and became the governor of Zhongdu in the State of Lu. He was conscientious and diligent in government affairs. With his governance, the people there lived in peace and stability. According to legend, Confucius also went fishing during his leisure time. He advocated fishing with a fishing rod instead of a net. Kind and righteous, he used his actions to teach his disciples to be temperate in everything and to know where to draw the line.

# 乐至则无怨，礼至则不争 ——《礼记》

　　乐可以调理人心，让人心情舒畅，没有怨恨；礼可以调理人的外在行为，让人们相互谦让，不起冲突。

When musical education does flourish, there will be no complaints. When ritual education does flourish, there will be no arguments.

*—The Book of Rites*

# 夹谷会盟

公元前 500 年夏，齐景公约鲁定公在一个叫夹谷的地方会面，孔子作为礼仪官参加了这次会面。其间，齐国企图绑架鲁定公，并胁迫鲁定公签署明显有利于齐国的协议，但都被孔子识破。这次会面齐景公不仅讨了个没趣，还被迫归还了鲁国被齐国侵占的土地。

# Meeting in Jiagu

In the summer of 500 BC, the Duke Jing of the State of Qi asked the Duke Ding of the State of Lu to meet in Jiagu. Confucius attended the meeting as a ceremonial officer. During the meeting, the Duke Jing of Qi planned to kidnap the Duke Ding of Lu and coerce him into signing an agreement that benefited Qi. However, Confucius saw through and resolved them one by one. In the end, the Duke Jing of Qi not only failed in his attempt, but also was forced to return the land occupied from Lu.

# 用之则行，舍之则藏 ——《论语》

如果用我，我就出来好好做事；如果不用我，我就藏起来好好过自己的生活。

When called to office, to undertake its duties;

When neglected, to be content to lead out a private life.

*—The Confucian Analects*

# 作《龟山操》

在孔子的治理下，鲁国的国力逐渐增强，这让齐国非常紧张。齐景公担心齐国的利益会因为鲁国而受到伤害，于是与鲁国当权派季氏合作，离间孔子与鲁定公的关系。孔子被迫离开鲁国。途中，孔子远眺家乡，龟山挡住了他的视线。在他看来，季氏家族跟眼前的龟山很像。孔子感伤正道衰微，同情百姓无处安身，于是创作古琴曲《龟山操》。

# Composing *Guishan Cao*

Under the governance of Confucius, the State of Lu gradually increased in power, which made the State of Qi very nervous. The Duke Jing of Qi worried that his state would be surpassed by Lu, so he cooperated with the ruling faction of Lu, the Ji family and drove a wedge between Confucius and the Duke Ding of Lu. Confucius had to leave Lu in the end. On the way away, Mount Gui blocked the view of Confucius overlooking his hometown. In his opinion, the Ji family was like Mount Gui in front of him. He wanted to go home, but he had no way to do it. Confucius lamented the decline of the righteous path and sympathized with the people's nowhere to settle down, so he wrote the Guqin music *Guishan Cao*.

# 三思而后行 ——《论语》

在采取行动之前，应该仔细思考可能的后果。

To think twice before you act.

——*The Confucian Analects*

# 临河返车

　　孔子带着弟子去晋国，打算投奔晋国的赵鞅。走到黄河边时，孔子听说赵鞅杀了贤臣窦鸣犊和舜华，他临河长叹："滔滔黄河看着真漂亮呀，只可惜我不能渡河了。"赵鞅不得志时得到了窦鸣犊、舜华二人的帮助，得志后就将二人杀害。孔子认为，自己去了晋国恐怕也会是同样的结局，于是驾车折返。

# Refusing to Work for the Unrighteous

　　Confucius took his disciples to the State of Jin to work for Zhao Yang. When they reached the Yellow River, Confucius heard that Zhao Yang had killed the virtuous officials Dou Mingdu and Shun Hua. Confucius sighed, "The surging Yellow River is so magnificent. However, I've decided not to cross it." When Zhao Yang hadn't achieved his ambition, he got the help from Dou Mingdu and Shun Hua, but he killed them soon after his aim had been achieved. Confucius thought that he would have the same outcome if he went to the State of Jin, so he went back.

# 道不同，不相为谋 ——《论语》

　　理想信念、学术见解等不同的人，没有必要一起谋划事情。

Those whose courses are different can not lay plans for one another.

　　　　　　　　　　　　—*The Confucian Analects*

# 宋人伐木

在宋国，孔子因批评执政大夫司马桓魋而惹怒了他。听说孔子经常在住处前面的大树下给弟子们讲学，桓魋派人砍掉了那棵大树，还让士兵去恐吓孔子。弟子劝孔子离开宋国，孔子说："老天让我有了这些德行，桓魋又能把我怎么样呢？"因不断传出桓魋要迫害孔子的消息，最终孔子扮成普通百姓离开了宋国。

# Huantui's Intimidation

In the State of Song, Confucius got into trouble for criticizing the ruling official Sima Huantui. Hearing that Confucius often gave lectures to his disciples under the big tree in front of his residence, Huantui sent someone to cut it down, and asked the soldiers to intimidate Confucius afterward. Disciples advised Confucius to leave Song, but Confucius said, "Heaven produced the virtue that is in me. Huantui, what can he do to me?" However, because of the constant news that Huantui was going to harm Confucius, Confucius finally disguised himself as an ordinary person and left.

# 人无远虑，必有近忧 ——《论语》

一个人如果没有做长远的考虑，那他必定会有眼前的忧患。

If a man takes no thought about what is distant, he will find sorrow near at hand.

— *The Confucian Analects*

# 丧家之犬

孔子周游列国期间，在到达郑国后与弟子们走散了。他独自一人站在郑国的东郭门外。一个郑国人告诉正在四处寻找孔子的子贡："东郭门外有个人，额头像尧，脖子像皋陶，肩膀像子产，自肩以下比禹短三寸，憔悴颓废的样子看上去就像是一只丧家之犬。"子贡找到孔子后，将此事告知孔子，孔子听后笑着说："他说的容貌不一定对，但他说我像丧家之犬却是对极了。"

# Homeless Dog

When Confucius traveled around all the states, he got separated from his disciples after arriving at the State of Zheng. Confucius stood alone outside the East Gate. A native told Zigong, a man who was looking for Confucius, "There is a man at the East Gate, who looks like a homeless dog, gaunt and dispirited, with a brain like Yao, a neck like Gaoyao, shoulders like Zichan, and three inches shorter than Dayu." When Zigong found Confucius and told it to him, Confucius laughed and said, "His words about my appearance may not be right, but he was right to say I was like a homeless dog."

# 三军可夺帅也，匹夫不可夺志也 　　——《论语》

　　军队的主帅可以被强行改变，但普通百姓的意志却不能被强行改变。

The commander of the forces of a large State may be carried off, but the will of even a common man cannot be taken from him.

—*The Confucian Analects*

# 雪后松柏

据说，孔子到陈国时正赶上楚国攻入陈国。楚军命令陈国的降兵修补西城门。降兵们备受屈辱，但孔子见了并没有对他们行礼致敬。孔子说："岁寒，然后知松柏之后凋也。"那些投降的士兵缺乏反抗的勇气和顽强的意志力，所以他们身上没有松柏那种骨气和大德。

# Pine and Cypress After Snow

As the story goes：The State of Chu occupied the State of Chen when Confucius arrived in Chen. The army of Chu ordered the surrendered soldiers to repair the West Gate. When Confucius saw it, he didn't give his salute to these surrendered soldiers. Confucius said, "Only when the weather turns cold, can we see that the leaves of pines and cypresses are the last to wither and fall, for pines and cypresses are strong enough to bear the severe cold after snow." In the war, soldiers who surrendered lacked the courage and willpower to resist. They did not have the backbone and virtue of the pine and the cypress.

# 小不忍则乱大谋 ——《论语》

    如果在小事上不能忍耐，那么就有可能败坏大事。

Want of forbearance in small matters confounds great plans.

                *—The Confucian Analects*

# 子见南子

孔子到卫国后，卫灵公的夫人南子派人约孔子见面，孔子告谢推辞。

后来，孔子不得已去见南子。进门后，孔子向北面恭敬地拱手行礼，南子在帷帐中还礼。一个多月后，卫灵公与南子出游，让孔子坐第二辆车招摇过市，孔子很是厌恶，于是离开了卫国。

# Meeting with Nanzi

When Confucius arrived in the State of Wei, Nanzi, the wife of the Duke Ling of Wei, sent someone to ask Confucius to meet her. Confucius refused.

Later, Confucius had to go to see Nanzi. After entering the door, Confucius performed the fist and palm salute respectfully to the north. Nanzi saluted in return to Confucius behind the curtain. More than a month later, the Duke Ling of Wei went on a trip with Nanzi. They let Confucius take the second coach to swagger through the city. Confucius was disgusted and left Wei.

# 德不孤，必有邻 ——《论语》

　　有道德的人不会孤单，定会有志同道
合的人与他做伴。

　　Virtue is not left to stand along. He who
practices it will have neighbors.

—The Confucian Analects

# 陈蔡绝粮

楚国派人聘请孔子，于是孔子带着弟子们前往楚国。陈、蔡两国的大夫们认为，如果孔子在楚国受到重用，那陈、蔡两国就危险了。于是在孔子等人途经陈、蔡两国的交界处时，他们派人将孔子师徒围了起来。孔子及其弟子被围困了七天，携带的粮食都吃光了，有些弟子甚至饿得都病倒了，但在此期间孔子弦诵不辍。直到子贡到楚国请来了救兵，他们才脱离困境。

# Predicament in Border

The State of Chu sent someone to invite Confucius, so he went to Chu with his disciples. The government officials of the State of Chen and the State of Cai thought if Confucius was put in an important post in Chu, Chen and Cai would be in danger. As a result, when Confucius and his disciples passed by the border of Chen and Cai, the two states sent soldiers to surround Confucius and his disciples. Confucius and his disciples were besieged for seven days and had nothing to eat in the end. Some disciples were so hungry that they were sick, but Confucius kept reciting and chanting. It was not until Zigong brought the reinforcements of Chu that they got out of the predicament.

# 德者本也，财者末也 ——《大学》

道德修养是一切的根本，而财富是细枝末节。

Virtue is the root; wealth is the result.

—*The Great Learning*

# 王者香

　　孔子周游列国，没有一个国家愿意重用他。从卫国返回鲁国的途中，在经过一个山谷时孔子看见了盛开的兰花。他深有感触地说："兰花应为王者香，现在却与众草为伍。这就好像有才华的人生不逢时，只能与学识浅薄的人为伍。"孔子停车赏兰，并取出古琴来创作了一曲《猗兰操》。此后，王者香成了中国兰花的别名。

# King of the Fragrant Plants

　　Confucius once traveled all the states, but no state was willing to use him. On the way back from the State of Wei to the State of Lu, Confucius saw orchids in full bloom when he passed through a valley. Confucius said with deep feeling, "The orchid should be the king of the fragrant plants, but now they grow together with weeds. It's like a talented person who can't fulfill his ambition and only associate with people with shallow knowledge." He stopped to admire orchids and took out the Guqin to create a piece of tune, *Yilan Cao*. Since then, the king of the fragrant plants has become another name for Chinese orchids.

## 诚于中，形于外 ——《大学》

内在的真实德性，一定会通过相应的外在行为表现出来。

What truly is within will be manifested without.

—*The Great Learning*

# 乌鸦护卫

　　据民间传说，孔子从尼山返回曲阜的路上遇见了歹人，孔子和弟子们寡不敌众，眼看就要抵挡不住。这时，不知从何处飞来了一大群乌鸦，它们啄散歹人并护送孔子等人回到孔府，之后就栖居在孔府附近。孔子逝世后，它们移居孔庙，继续守护孔庙。这群乌鸦忠心守护孔子，因此被后人称为"孔圣人的三千乌鸦兵"。

# The Crow Guards

　　According to folklore, Confucius once met a group of villains on his way back to Qufu from Mount Ni. Confucius and his disciples were outnumbered and could hardly resist. At this time, a large group of crows flew from nowhere. They pecked at the villains and escorted Confucius and his disciples back to the Confucius Family Mansion. Then they lived near the Confucius Family Mansion. After the death of Confucius, the crows moved to the Temple of Confucius and continued to guard the temple. Because their loyalty to Confucius, they were called the "three thousand crow soldiers of Confucius" by later generations.

# 人能弘道，非道弘人 ——《论语》

人能使道发扬光大，而不是道能使人的才能扩大。

A man can enlarge the principles which he follows;
those principles do not enlarge the man.

—*The Confucian Analects*

# 遇麟绝笔

公元前 481 年，叔孙氏的车夫在大野狩猎时打死了一头野兽。那野兽看上去像獐子，头上却有一对肉角，十分罕见，因此大家都认为它是不祥之物。冉有将此事告知了孔子，71 岁的孔子在弟子的搀扶下赶了过去。当看到被猎杀的野兽是神兽麒麟时，孔子神情悲愤，哭着说："这是麒麟啊，麒麟是仁兽，它一出现就被杀害了，看来我奉行的主张无法实现了。"悲从心来，事后孔子写下绝笔之作《春秋》。

# The Last Work
## —The Spring and Autumn Annals

In 481 BC, Shusun's coachman hunted a beast in the wild. The beast, which was rarely seen, looked like a roe but had a pair of horns on its head. It was considered unlucky by people. Ranyou told Confucius about it. The 71-year-old Confucius hurried over with the help of his disciples. Confucius looked sad and angry when he saw the beast hunted was a kylin. Confucius said, "This is a kylin, a benevolent animal. It was killed as soon as it appeared. It seems that my proposition won't be realized." Confucius was very sad and wrote his last work, *The Spring and Autumn Annals*.

# 画述孔子故乡遗迹风情

## Paintings of the Relics and Customs
## in Confucius' Hometown

# 孔府

孔府是世袭"衍圣公"
的府邸。孔府内的重光门得
名于明嘉靖皇帝御赐的匾额
"恩赐重光"。

# The Confucius Family Mansion

The Confucius Family Mansion is the residence of "Duke Yansheng", a special honor given to the direct descendant of Confucius. The Chongguang Gate in the Mansion is named after the plaque "Mercy on Chongguang" bestowed by the Emperor Jiajing of Ming Dynasty.

# 孔庙

　　孔庙位于曲阜市中心，是祭祀孔子和展示儒家思想的场所。孔庙内有一座单孔石拱桥，桥东西各有一棵古柏树，人称"二柏担一孔"。

# The Temple of Confucius

　　The Temple of Confucius is located in the center of Qufu City. It is the place to offer sacrifice to Confucius and demonstrate Confucianism. In the temple, there is a single-span stone arch bridge with one old cypress on each side. It is called "two cypresses shouldering the bridge".

# 孔林

　　孔林位于曲阜城北 1.5 千米处，是孔子及其后裔的墓地所在。孔林有超过 10 万座墓地，是世界上规模最大、存续时间最长的家族墓地。

# The Cemetery of Confucius

    The Cemetery of Confucius is located in 1.5 kilometers north of Qufu City. As the cemetery of Confucius and his descendants, there are more than 100 000 tombs. The Cemetery has become the largest family cemetery with the longest duration in the world.

# 尼山圣境

尼山圣境位于曲阜市东南 25 千米处，是一个集文化体验、修学启智、生态旅游、休闲度假于一体的复合型文化度假产业综合体。

# Nishan Sacred Land

The Nishan Sacred Land is located in 25 kilometers southeast of Qufu City. It is a complex cultural holiday industry integrating cultural experience, learning and enlightenment, ecotourism and leisure vacation.

# 孔子生迹园

　　孔子生迹园位于孔林南 100 米处，是一个
以展示孔子生平为主的儒家文化园区。

# The Park of Confucius

The Park of Confucius is located at 100 meters south of the
Cemetery of Confucius. It is a park that mainly displays the life of
Confucius.

# 颜母祠

　　颜母祠原位于孔子母亲颜徵在的故乡颜母
庄村，是后人为了纪念孔子母亲而建的。

# The Temple of Yanmu

The Temple of Yanmu was originally located at Yanmuzhuang Village, the hometown of Confucius' mother, Yan Zhengzai. It was built by later generations in memory of her.

# 夫子洞

相传夫子洞是孔子的出生之地，位于曲阜市尼山脚下的一处石壁中。

# The Fuzi Cave

According to the legend, the Fuzi Cave is where Confucius was born. With stone as its walls, it is located at the foot of Mount Ni in Qufu City.

# 石门山

石门山位于曲阜城东
北 25 千米处，是国家级森
林公园。据说孔子在此完
成了一部分对《周易》的
注解工作。

# Mount Shimen

Mount Shimen, located in 25 kilometers northeast of Qufu City, is a national forest park. It is said that part of the annotating work of *The Book of Changes* by Confucius was completed here.

# 九仙山

九仙山位于曲阜市吴村镇，传说是九个仙女下凡变成的。孔子及其弟子曾登临九仙山。

# Mount Jiuxian

Mount Jiuxian are located in Wucun Town, Qufu City. Legend has it that nine immortals came down to the earth and turned into Mount Jiuxian. Confucius and his disciples once visited Mount Jiuxian.

# 峄山

# Mount Yi

峄山位于曲阜以南33千米处。据说孔子多次登临峄山，并在峄山上为弟子们授课。

Mount Yi is located in 33 kilometers south of Qufu City. It is said that Confucius visited Mount Yi many times and gave lessons to his disciples there.

# 孔子湖

孔子湖位于曲阜市尼山镇，因孔子诞生在
尼山而得名。

# Confucius Lake

Confucius Lake is located in Nishan Town, Qufu City. The town is named after Mount Ni, the birthplace of Confucius.

# 大沂河

　　大沂河是曲阜的第二大河流。孔子及其弟
子游憩的舞雩台就位于河的北岸。

# Dayi River

The Dayi River is the second largest river in Qufu. The Rain Altar where Confucius once lectured and rested is by the north side of the river.

# 泗河

孔子曾在泗河旁感叹，时间就像这流水一样，一去不复返。在曲阜城东北 4 千米的泗河南岸，有孔子讲学的洙泗书院。

# Si River

Confucius once lamented by the Si River that like the running water, time never returns. On the south bank of the Si River, 4 kilometers northeast of Qufu City, there was Zhusi Academy where Confucius taught.

# 扳倒井

扳倒井现位于邹城市宋家山头村内。据说孔母曾将井扳倒，取水饮用。

# The Tilted Well

The Tilted Well is now located at the village of Songjiashantou, Zoucheng City. It is said that Confucius' mother once pulled down the well to get water to drink.

# 古泮池

古泮池位于曲阜明故城东南隅，相传是孔
子和弟子们的休憩之地。

## Ancient Panchi

The Ancient Panchi is located in the southeast corner of the Qufu
Ming Dynasty Ancient City. It is said that Confucius and his disciples
used to rest here.

# 蓼河公园

蓼河公园是曲阜市的一处特色生态景区，
孔子博物馆就坐落在蓼河公园以北。

# Liaohe Park

The Liaohe Park is an ecotourist attraction in Qufu City. The Confucius Museum is located on the north of the Liaohe Park.

# 孟庙

孟庙是人们祭祀孟子的场所。孟庙内立有一块"母教一人"的石碑。

# The Temple of Mencius

The Temple of Mencius is the place for people to worship Mencius. There is a monument inside the temple, where it says "Mencius' mother is the first mother to succeed in family education in the history of China".

# 颜庙

颜庙位于曲阜市陋巷街北首，是供奉孔子弟子颜回的祠庙。因颜回被后人尊为复圣，故颜庙也被叫作复圣庙。

# The Temple of Yan Hui

The Temple of Yan Hui is located at the north end of Louxiang Street in Qufu City. It is the temple dedicated to Yan Hui, the favorite disciple of Confucius. Because Yan Hui is honored by later generations as Fusheng, the Temple of Yan Hui is also called the Temple of Fusheng.

奋發向上
庚子年八月
沣墨吳海

## 鲤鱼

　　为了避孔鲤的名字之讳，
在孔子故乡，人们将鲤鱼叫作
红鱼。

# Carp

In order to taboo the name of Kong Li,
people in Confucius' hometown give carp
another name, red fish.

## 麒麟窗花

# Traceries with Kylin

因为麒麟送子的传说，人们敬畏麒麟。在曲阜，家中有孩子降生时有贴麒麟窗花庆祝的习俗。

Because of the legend of kylin delivering the sage, people revere the kylin. When a child is born, it is customary to paste traceries with kylin to celebrate in Qufu.

# 腊肉

# Cured Meat

据说，就因为孔子曾说只要有人带给他十块腊肉，他就可以收那人为弟子，所以在孔子的故乡形成了过年做腊肉的习俗。

It is said that Confucius once said that if someone brought him ten pieces of cured meat, he would take him as a disciple. Gradually, the custom of making cured meat during the Spring Festival came into being in Confucius' hometown.

# 兰花

兰花是曲阜市的市花，人们常用成语"芝兰之室"来比喻良好的环境。

# Orchids

The orchid is the floral emblem of Qufu. People often use the idiom "a room full of fragrance of orchids" to describe a morally fine environment.

# 作者简介

　　吴冰，艺名泮墨。1984年毕业于上海大学文学院历史系，毕业后就职于上海博物馆。1994年日本京都教育大学艺术系研究生毕业，2012年被聘为上海大学考古与文物研究中心兼职研究员。目前是香港泮墨画院院长，曲阜泮墨美术馆馆长，孔子生迹园文化旅游景区的创建者。

　　吴冰自幼习画，几十年来一直致力于中国古代文化与书画艺术的研究，凭着扎实的绘画功底和较为深厚的中国传统文化的底蕴，他形成了个人独特的艺术风格，是位集文学、艺术于一体的跨界文化学者型画家。

# About the Author

Wu Bing, whose stage name is Pan Mo, graduated from the History Department of the School of Literature, Shanghai University in 1984, and worked in the Shanghai Museum after graduation. In 1994, he graduated with a master's degree from the Art Department of Kyoto University of Education, Japan, and in 2012, he was engaged as a part-time researcher at the Archaeology and Cultural Relics Research Center of Shanghai University. Currently, he is the director of Hong Kong Panmo Painting Academy, the director of Qufu Panmo Art Museum, and the founder of the Park of Confucius.

Wu Bing has studied painting since childhood and has devoted himself to the study of ancient Chinese culture and calligraphy and painting art for decades. With painting skills and Chinese traditional cultural heritage, he has formed a unique artistic style. Combining art with literature, he now is a scholarly painter.